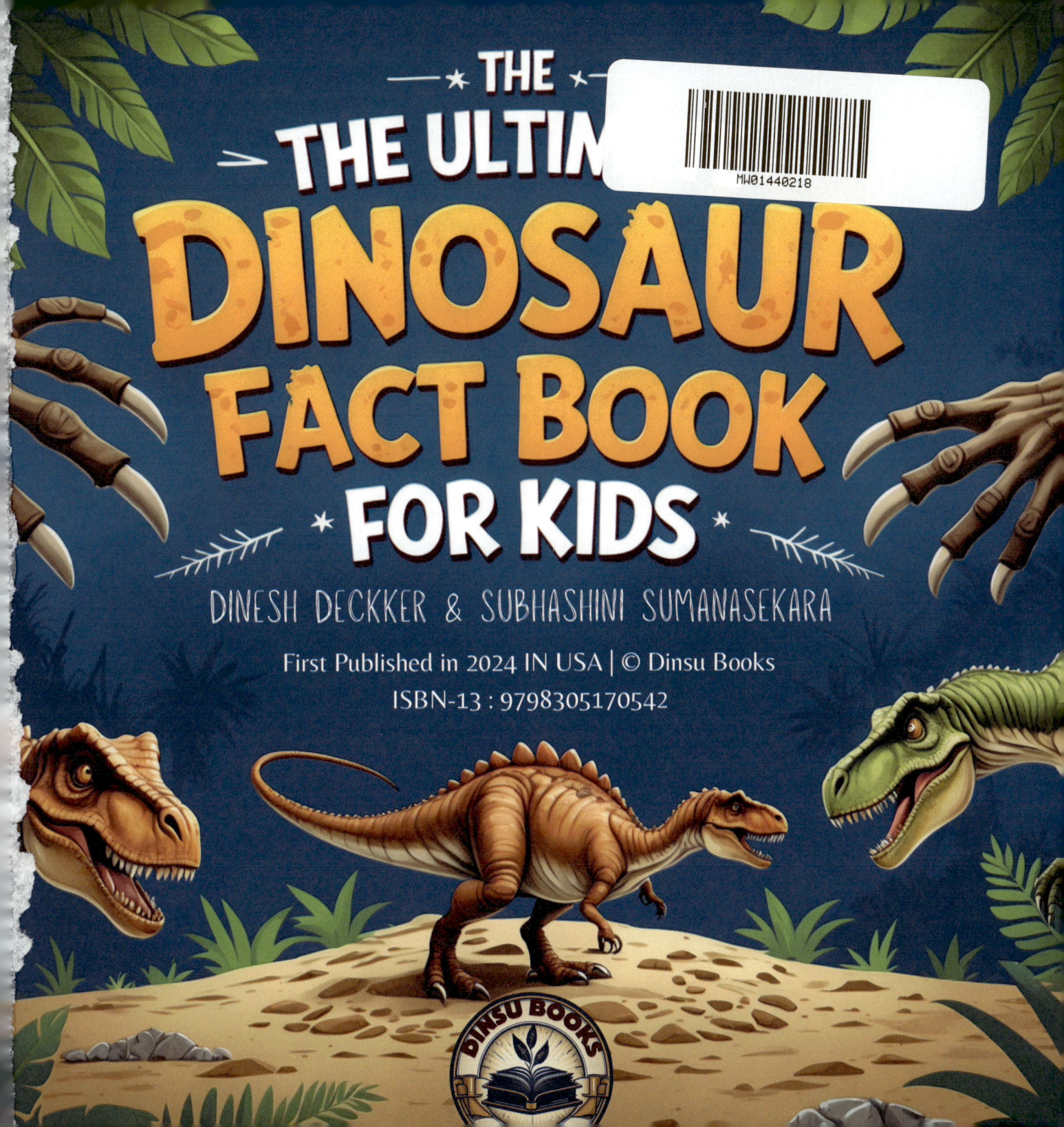

THE ULTIMATE DINOSAUR FACT BOOK FOR KIDS

DINESH DECKKER & SUBHASHINI SUMANASEKARA

First Published in 2024 IN USA | © Dinsu Books

ISBN-13 : 9798305170542

THE ULTIMATE
DINOSAUR FACT BOOK FOR KIDS

1	WHAT ARE DINOSAURS?	04
2	TYPES OF DINOSAURS	09
3	THE DINO TIMELINE	16
4	DINOSAUR SUPERPOWERS	55
5	HOW DID DINOSAURS DISAPPEAR?	62
6	DINOSAURS IN OUR WORLD	76
7	QUIZZES & EXPERIMENTS	83

Introduction:
Welcome to the World of Dinosaurs!

Dear Dino Explorers,
Get ready to embark on a time-traveling adventure to a world unlike anything you've ever imagined—a world where gigantic plant-eaters roamed lush forests, swift hunters raced across open plains, and the skies were ruled by creatures with wings wider than a bus! Welcome to the Age of Dinosaurs.

In this book, we'll explore everything you've ever wanted to know about dinosaurs:

- What they looked like, how they lived, and why they disappeared.
- The incredible superpowers that made them the kings and queens of their world.
- How scientists uncover their secrets millions of years later.

Along the way, you'll discover fun facts, answer quizzes, and even try hands-on activities that will make you feel like a real paleontologist. Whether you're a fan of the fierce T. rex, the gentle Brachiosaurus, or the clever Velociraptor, there's something here for every dino lover.

So grab your gear, put on your explorer hat, and let's dive into the prehistoric past. Adventure awaits—let's make history come alive!

Let's go!
Your Dino Guide

Chapter 1: What Are Dinosaurs?

Welcome to the world of dinosaurs—the most amazing creatures to ever stomp across the Earth! But wait... What exactly are dinosaurs?

Dinosaurs were reptiles, just like today's lizards and snakes, but WAY bigger and cooler (sorry, lizards). These fascinating creatures lived millions of years ago during the Mesozoic Era—also called the Age of Dinosaurs.

Dino Fact-o-Meter

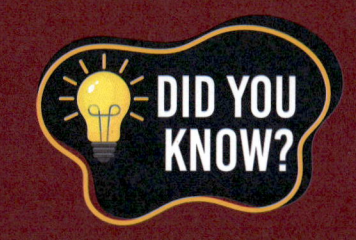

The word dinosaur comes from two Greek words: deinos (terrible) and sauros (lizard). But don't worry, they weren't all terrible. Some were tiny and friendly plant-eaters!

The word dinosaur comes from two Greek words: deinos (terrible) and sauros (lizard). But don't worry, they weren't all terrible. Some were tiny and friendly plant-eaters!

DID YOU KNOW?

How Big Were They?

Let's talk size! Dinosaurs came in all shapes and sizes. The Argentinosaurus was as long as three school buses parked end to end—imagine the traffic jam! On the other hand, the tiny Microraptor could fit in your hands. That's right—a flying dino as small as a bird! On the other hand, the tiny Microraptor could fit in your hands. That's right—a flying dino as small as a bird!

40M

FUN FACT

77CM

Did You Know?

Some dinosaurs weren't scary at all. Plant-eaters like Triceratops had big, strong horns, but they only used them to protect themselves. It's like carrying a shield wherever you go!

ACTIVITY

Grab a measuring tape and mark 40 feet on the ground. That's how long the famous Tyrannosaurus rex could be! Now imagine it stomping down your street. Would you run, or would you wave hello?

Chapter 2: Types of Dinosaurs

Dinosaurs weren't all giant meat-eating monsters (although some were). They came in all shapes, sizes, and personalities. Let's meet some of the coolest dinos from each category!

1. Herbivores:
The Plant Munchers

2. Carnivores:
The Meat Munchers

3. Omnivores:
The All-You-Can-Eaters

1. Herbivores: The Plant Munchers

These dinos were the vegetarians of the prehistoric world. They loved munching on leaves, ferns, and even bark!

Triceratops

With three sharp horns and a frill as big as a shield, this dino looked like a walking tank. But don't worry. Triceratops only used its horns for defense or to impress other dinos.

💡 Its frill could be over 6 feet wide! That's taller than your bedroom door.

Brachiosaurus

This gentle giant had a neck so long it could nibble leaves from the tallest trees—no ladder needed!

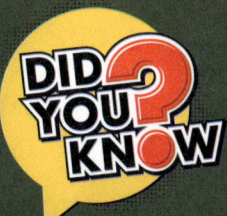

DID YOU KNOW? Brachiosaurus weighed as much as four elephants. That's a LOT of salad.

Stegosaurus

Famous for the row of spiky plates on its back, Stegosaurus looked like it was ready for battle. But it used its spiky tail, called a "thagomizer," to scare off predators.

DID YOU KNOW? Its brain was the size of a walnut. Small brain, big personality!

2. Carnivores: The Meat Munchers

These fearsome predators ruled the food chain with sharp teeth and fast moves.

Tyrannosaurus rex
The king of dinosaurs! With jaws that could crush bones and teeth as long as bananas, T. rex was a dino you wouldn't want to mess with.

A T. REX could run up to 20 miles per hour. Imagine being chased by one on a bike—yikes!

Velociraptor

These speedy hunters were small but fierce, hunting in packs to take down bigger prey. They even had sharp claws shaped like sickles!

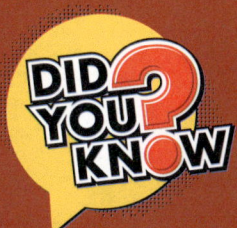

DID YOU KNOW? Velociraptors weren't as big as in the movies they were only about the size of a turkey.

Spinosaurus

Bigger than T. rex and with a sail-like fin on its back, Spinosaurus was a fish-loving dino that hunted in rivers.

DID YOU KNOW? It's the first known swimming dinosaur!

3. Omnivores: The All-You-Can-Eaters 🍗🍖

Why choose between plants and meat when you can have both? Omnivores had the best of both worlds.

Oviraptor
Its name means "egg thief," but this little dino probably just liked a varied diet of plants, small animals, and yes, maybe the occasional egg.

💡 Oviraptors had feathers—yes, feathers! Some looked like colorful prehistoric birds.

Troodon

Troodon was small, smart, and had big eyes perfect for spotting food at night. It could eat plants, meat, or even bugs!

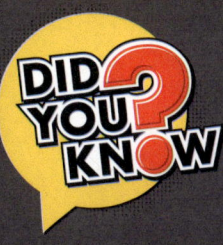

DID YOU KNOW? Troodon is considered one of the smartest dinosaurs, with a brain-to-body size ratio similar to modern birds.

Dino Detective Quiz

Can you guess which type of dinosaur these clues describe?
1. I have three horns, but I don't eat meat. Who am I?
2. I swim in rivers and have a big sail on my back. Who am I?
3. I hunt in packs and have claws like sickles. Who am I?

Chapter 3: The Dino Timeline

Dinosaurs ruled the Earth for a REALLY long time—about 165 million years! That's so long, it's hard to imagine. To make it easier, scientists divide this time into three big chapters called the Triassic, Jurassic, and Cretaceous periods. Let's travel back in time and explore each one!

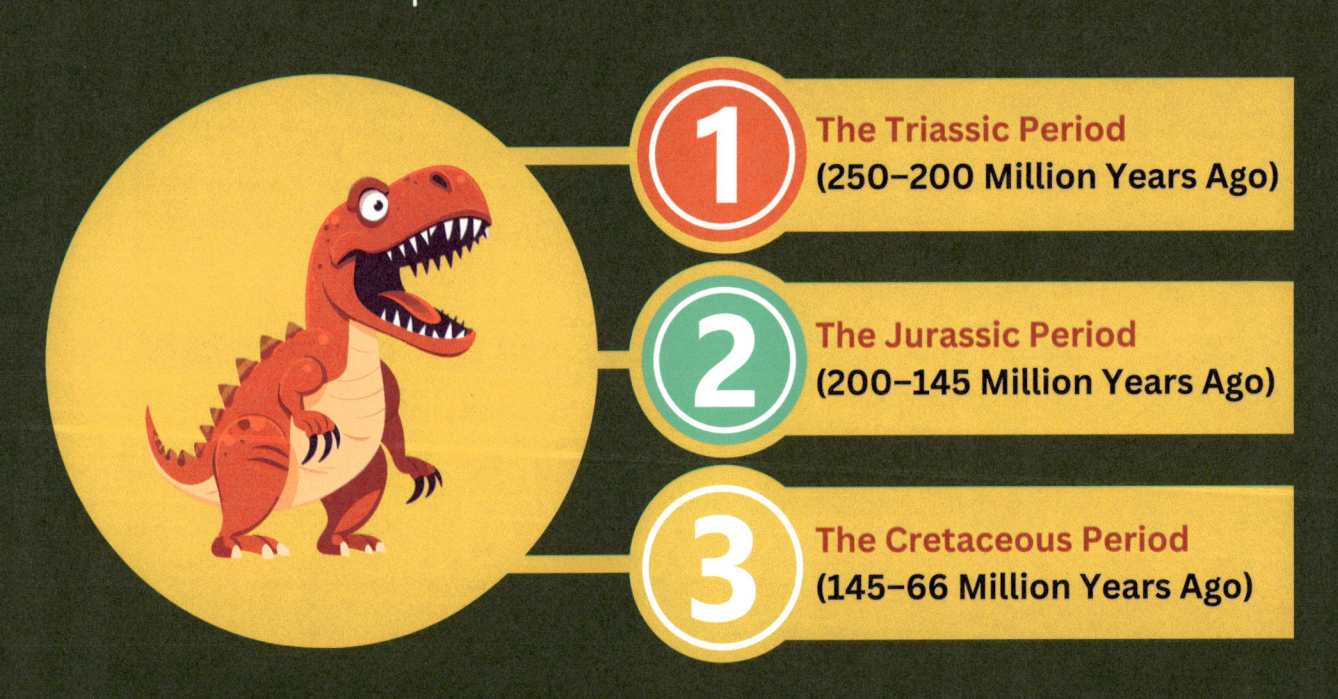

1 **The Triassic Period**
(250–200 Million Years Ago)

2 **The Jurassic Period**
(200–145 Million Years Ago)

3 **The Cretaceous Period**
(145–66 Million Years Ago)

1. THE TRIASSIC PERIOD
(250–200 Million Years Ago)

Welcome to the dawn of dinosaurs! The Earth looked very different back then—there was one big supercontinent called Pangaea, and the climate was hot and dry.

The First Dinosaurs Appear!
Dinosaurs were small and speedy at first, like the chicken-sized Eoraptor. They weren't the top predators yet; they had to compete with crocodile-like creatures and other reptiles.

FUN FACT
Dinosaurs were small and speedy at first, like the chicken-sized Eoraptor. They weren't the top predators yet; they had to compete with crocodile-like creatures and other reptiles.

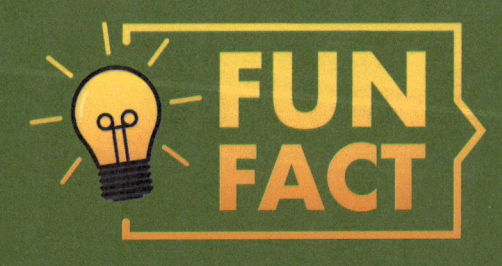

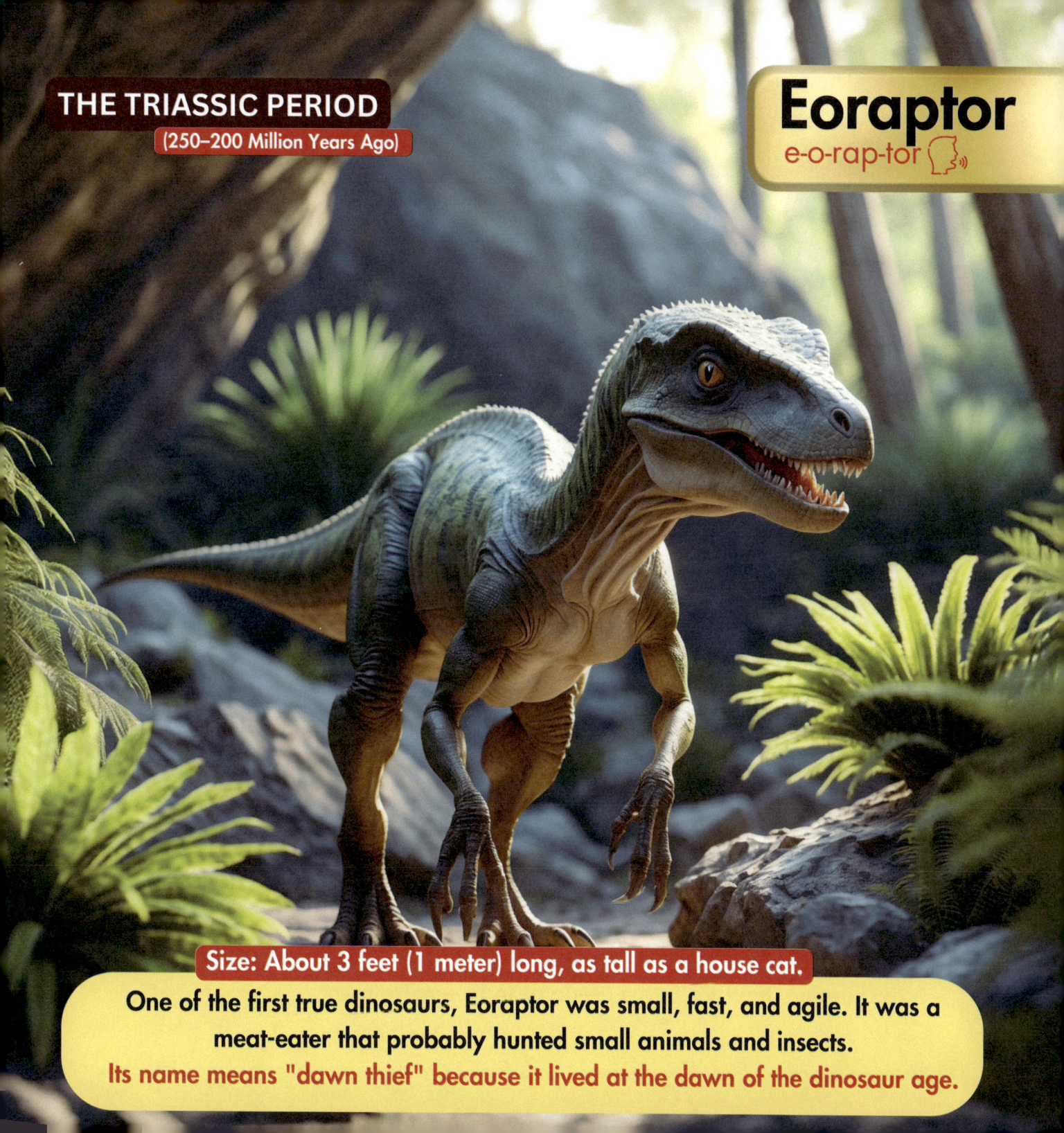

THE TRIASSIC PERIOD
(250–200 Million Years Ago)

Eoraptor
e-o-rap-tor

Size: About 3 feet (1 meter) long, as tall as a house cat.

One of the first true dinosaurs, Eoraptor was small, fast, and agile. It was a meat-eater that probably hunted small animals and insects.
Its name means "dawn thief" because it lived at the dawn of the dinosaur age.

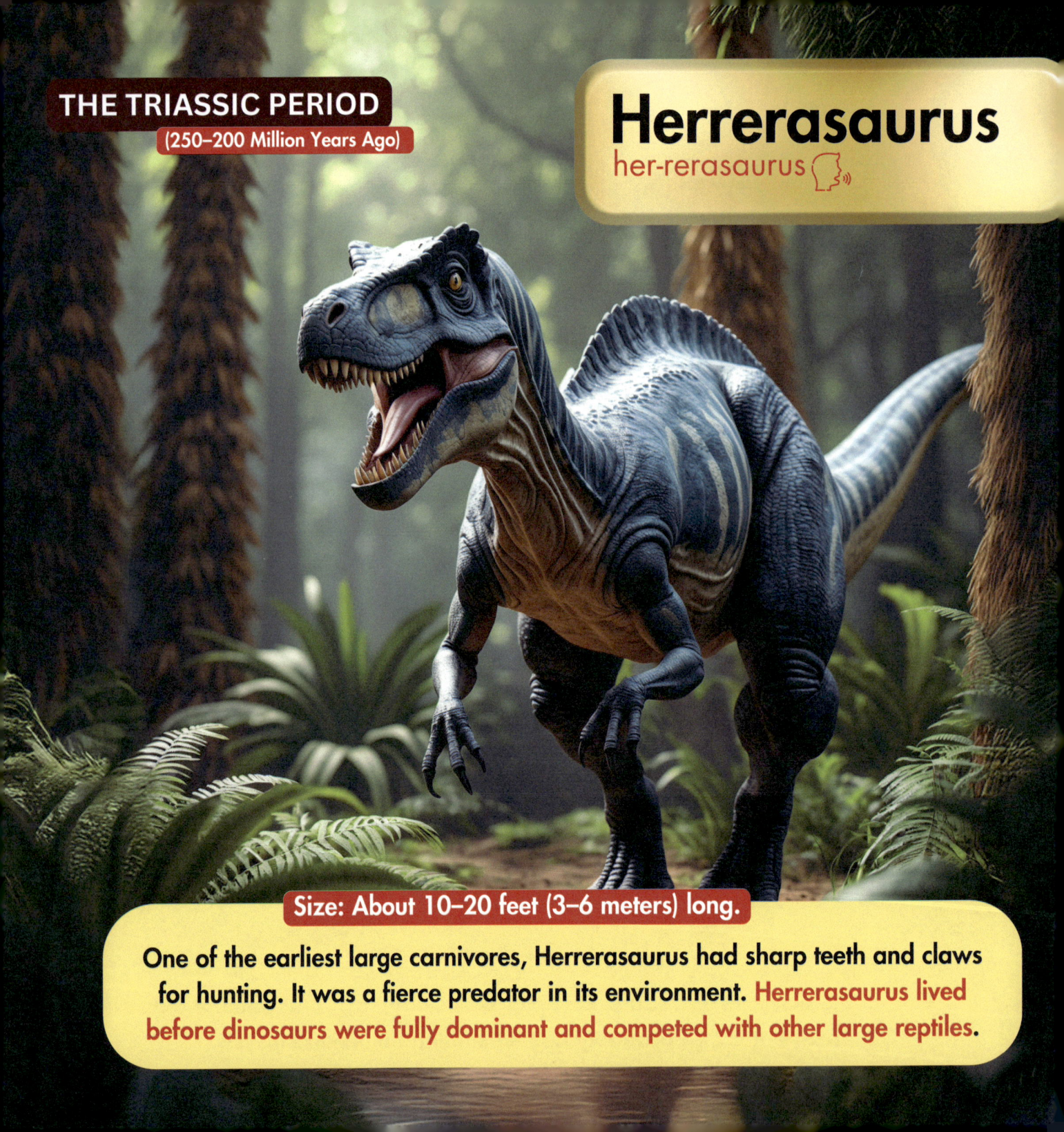

THE TRIASSIC PERIOD
(250–200 Million Years Ago)

Herrerasaurus
her-rerasaurus

Size: About 10–20 feet (3–6 meters) long.

One of the earliest large carnivores, Herrerasaurus had sharp teeth and claws for hunting. It was a fierce predator in its environment. *Herrerasaurus lived before dinosaurs were fully dominant and competed with other large reptiles.*

THE TRIASSIC PERIOD
(250–200 Million Years Ago)

Plateosaurus
plat-ee-oh-sore-us

About 30 feet (9 meters) long.

A plant-eater with a long neck and a bulky body, Plateosaurus was an early member of the sauropodomorph group, which later evolved into giants like Brachiosaurus. Plateosaurus could walk on two or four legs, depending on the situation.

THE TRIASSIC PERIOD
(250–200 Million Years Ago)

Coelophysis
See-low-fy-sis

Size: About 9 feet (3 meters) long.

A small, lightweight carnivore, Coelophysis was a fast runner that hunted in packs. It had sharp teeth and excellent vision. **Coelophysis fossils are often found in groups, suggesting it lived and hunted in packs.**

THE TRIASSIC PERIOD
(250–200 Million Years Ago)

Mussaurus
moo-sawr-us

Size: Babies about 8 inches (20 cm) and Grow up to 10 feet (3 meters).

A tiny, early herbivore, Mussaurus means "mouse lizard." Despite its name, adults were much larger than a mouse! Mussaurus is known for its tiny baby fossils, some of the smallest dinosaur fossils ever found.

THE TRIASSIC PERIOD
(250–200 Million Years Ago)

Nyasasaurus
nye-as-suh-sore-us

Size: About 6.5 feet (2 meters) long.

Possibly the earliest dinosaur or dinosaur-like creature, Nyasasaurus is a mysterious species that bridges the gap between early reptiles and true dinosaurs. Fossils of Nyasasaurus were discovered in Tanzania, near Lake Nyasa (now called Lake Malawi), which inspired its name.

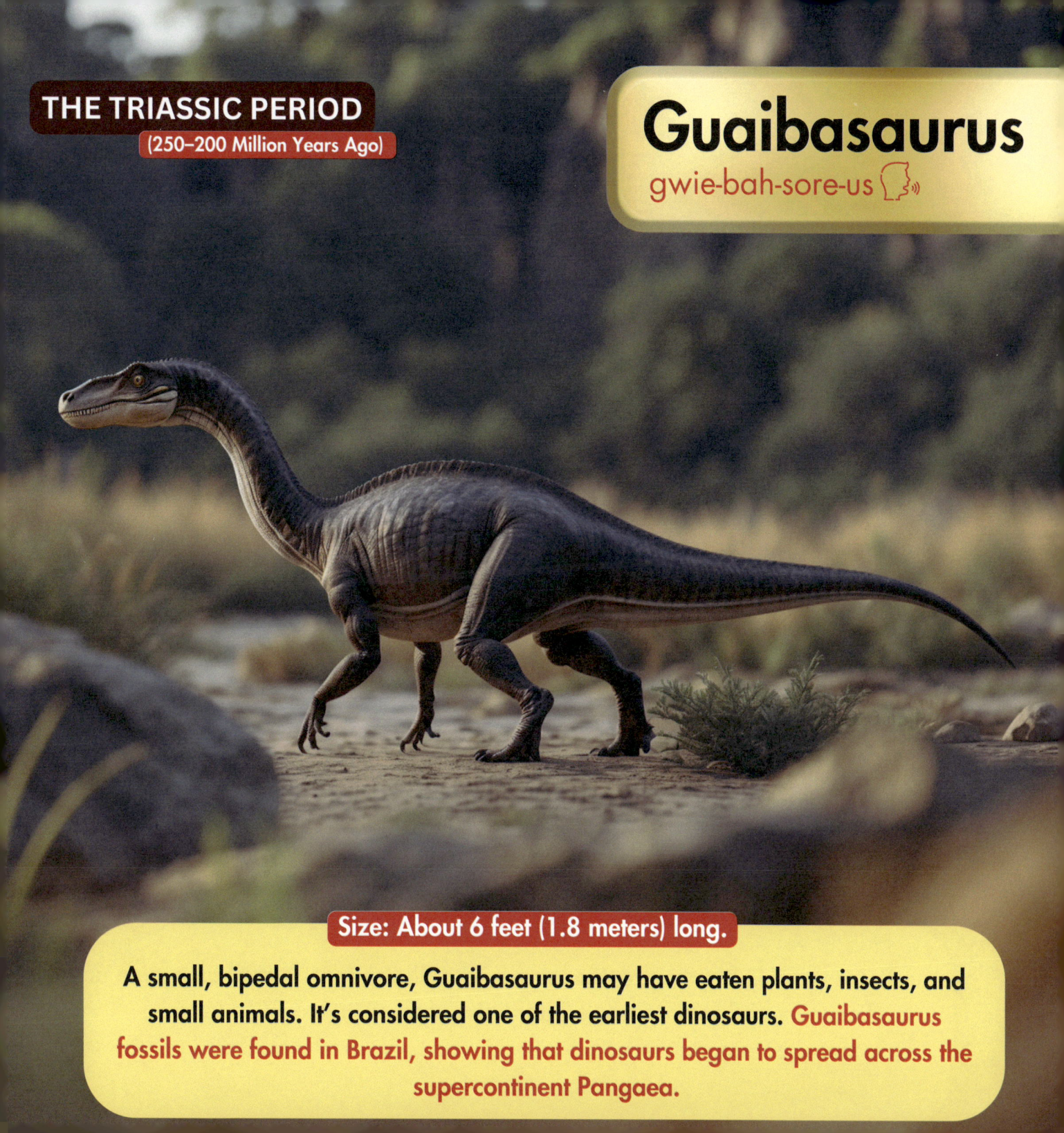

THE TRIASSIC PERIOD
(250–200 Million Years Ago)

Guaibasaurus
gwie-bah-sore-us

Size: About 6 feet (1.8 meters) long.

A small, bipedal omnivore, Guaibasaurus may have eaten plants, insects, and small animals. It's considered one of the earliest dinosaurs. Guaibasaurus fossils were found in Brazil, showing that dinosaurs began to spread across the supercontinent Pangaea.

Ischigualastia

is-chigualas-ti-a

THE TRIASSIC PERIOD
(250–200 Million Years Ago)

Size: About 13 feet (4 meters) long.

A massive, plant-eating reptile known as a dicynodont, it lived alongside early dinosaurs and could grow to impressive sizes. While not a true dinosaur, it competed with early dinos for resources, giving a glimpse into the Triassic ecosystem.

THE TRIASSIC PERIOD
(250–200 Million Years Ago)

Liliensternus
lil-ee-en-shtern-us

Size: About 17 feet (5 meters) long.

A slender, bipedal predator with sharp teeth and a long tail, Liliensternus was one of the largest carnivores of the Triassic Period. *It's named after Hugo Rühle von Lilienstern, a German paleontologist who studied early dinosaur fossils.*

THE TRIASSIC PERIOD
(250–200 Million Years Ago)

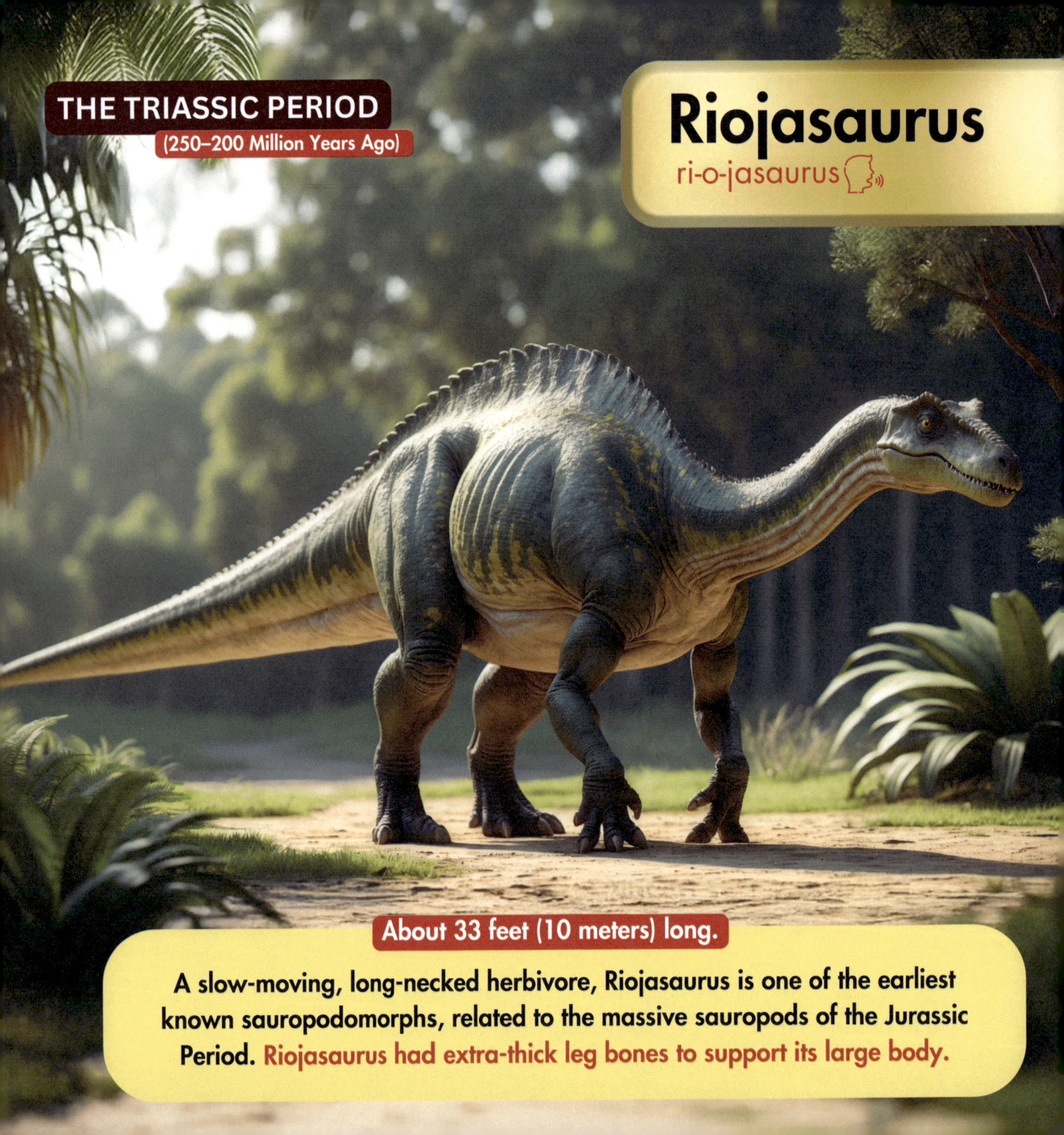

Riojasaurus
ri-o-jasaurus

About 33 feet (10 meters) long.

A slow-moving, long-necked herbivore, Riojasaurus is one of the earliest known sauropodomorphs, related to the massive sauropods of the Jurassic Period. Riojasaurus had extra-thick leg bones to support its large body.

2. THE JURASSIC PERIOD

(200–145 Million Years Ago)

Cue the theme music—this is the time of the giants! Dinosaurs grew larger and more diverse as the climate became warm and wet, with lush forests full of food.

The Age of Giants
This was when enormous plant-eaters like Brachiosaurus and Diplodocus roamed the land, chomping on treetops. They were so big that even predators thought twice before attacking.

Meet the Superstars
Carnivores like Allosaurus became the dominant predators, while the first birds, like Archaeopteryx, began to flap their feathered wings.

Did You Know?

Did you know the famous Stegosaurus lived during this time? Its brain was so small, it weighed only as much as a lime!

THE JURASSIC PERIOD
(200–145 Million Years Ago)

Brachiosaurus
brae·kee·uh·saw·ruhs

About 85 feet (26 meters) long and 40 feet (12 meters) tall.

A long-necked, towering herbivore that used its height to munch on treetop leaves. **Unlike most long-necked dinosaurs, Brachiosaurus had longer front legs, giving it a giraffe-like stance.**

THE JURASSIC PERIOD
(200–145 Million Years Ago)

Stegosaurus
steh·guh·saw·ruhs

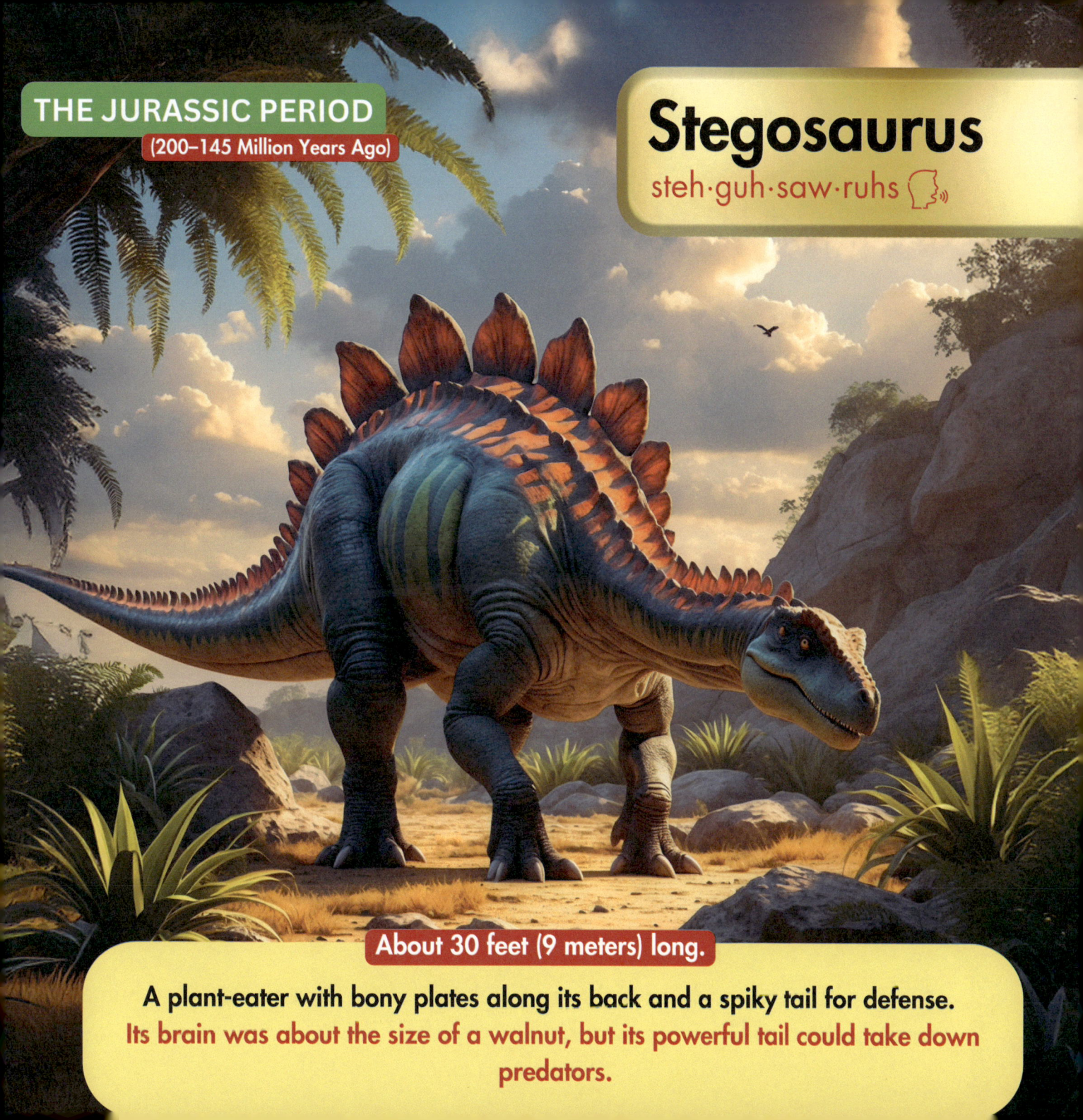

About 30 feet (9 meters) long.

A plant-eater with bony plates along its back and a spiky tail for defense. Its brain was about the size of a walnut, but its powerful tail could take down predators.

THE JURASSIC PERIOD
(200–145 Million Years Ago)

Allosaurus
al-oh-sor-uhss

Size: About 30 feet (9 meters) long.

A fierce carnivore and one of the top predators of the Jurassic Period, it hunted large herbivores like Stegosaurus. Allosaurus had sharp, serrated teeth perfect for tearing meat.

THE JURASSIC PERIOD
(200–145 Million Years Ago)

Diplodocus
duh·plo·duh·kuhs

Size: About 90 feet (27 meters) long.

A long-necked, whip-tailed herbivore that grazed on low-lying plants. Diplodocus could use its long tail like a whip for defense against predators.

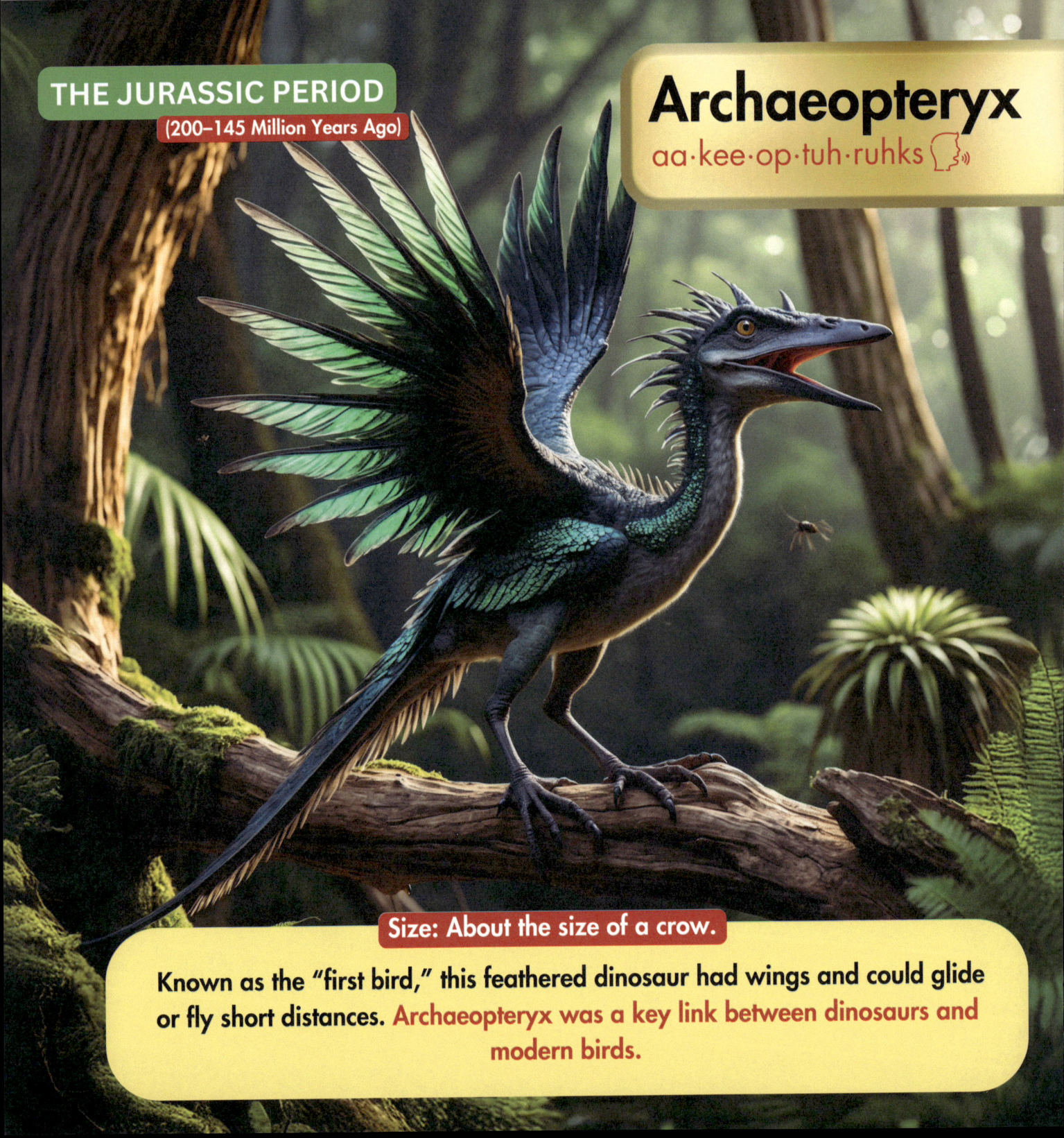

THE JURASSIC PERIOD
(200–145 Million Years Ago)

Archaeopteryx
aa·kee·op·tuh·ruhks

Size: About the size of a crow.

Known as the "first bird," this feathered dinosaur had wings and could glide or fly short distances. **Archaeopteryx was a key link between dinosaurs and modern birds.**

Camarasaurus
cam·a·ra·sau·rus

THE JURASSIC PERIOD
(200–145 Million Years Ago)

Size: About 50 feet (15 meters) long.

A large, plant-eating dinosaur with a sturdy body and a short neck compared to other sauropods. Its name means "chambered lizard" because of the hollow spaces in its bones.

THE JURASSIC PERIOD
(200–145 Million Years Ago)

Ceratosaurus
cer-ato-saurus

Size: About 20 feet (6 meters) long.

A medium-sized carnivore with a horn on its nose and blade-like teeth for cutting meat. Ceratosaurus was a great swimmer, which gave it an edge in hunting.

Apatosaurus
ap-ato-saurus

THE JURASSIC PERIOD
(200–145 Million Years Ago)

Size: About 75 feet (23 meters) long.

A massive sauropod with a long neck and tail that helped it reach food in trees and fend off predators. Its name means "deceptive lizard" because scientists initially misclassified its fossils.

THE JURASSIC PERIOD
(200–145 Million Years Ago)

Compsognathus
komp·sog·nuh·thuhs 🗣

Size: About the size of a chicken.

A small, fast-moving carnivore that likely fed on insects and small lizards. Its fossils are so well-preserved that scientists know what it ate for its last meal!

Barosaurus
baro-saurus

THE JURASSIC PERIOD
(200–145 Million Years Ago)

Size: About 80 feet (24 meters) long.

A massive sauropod closely related to Diplodocus, known for its incredibly long neck. **Barosaurus had one of the longest necks of any dinosaur—up to 30 feet (9 meters).**

3. THE CRETACEOUS PERIOD
(200–145 Million Years Ago)

This was the golden age of dinosaurs, with more species than ever before! Flowering plants appeared for the first time, and the continents started to drift apart, creating new environments for dinos to thrive.

The Reign of T. Rex
This period gave us some of the most famous dinos, like Tyrannosaurus rex, Triceratops, and Velociraptor.

The Feathered Revolution
Many dinosaurs, especially smaller ones, had feathers, showing how closely they were related to modern birds.

The Big Goodbye
The Cretaceous ended with a bang—literally. A giant asteroid hit the Earth, causing massive fires, dust clouds, and climate change. This wiped out most dinosaurs, except for their bird relatives.

Fun Fact
The asteroid impact left a crater in Mexico's Yucatán Peninsula that's over 90 miles wide. That's as long as 1,440 football fields lined up!

THE CRETACEOUS PERIOD
(200–145 Million Years Ago)

Tyrannosaurus rex
tai·ra·nuh·saw·ruhs reks

Size: About 40 feet (12 meters) long and 15 feet (4.5 meters) tall.

The "king of dinosaurs," T. rex was a massive predator with powerful jaws and sharp teeth. T. rex's bite was so strong it could crush bones!

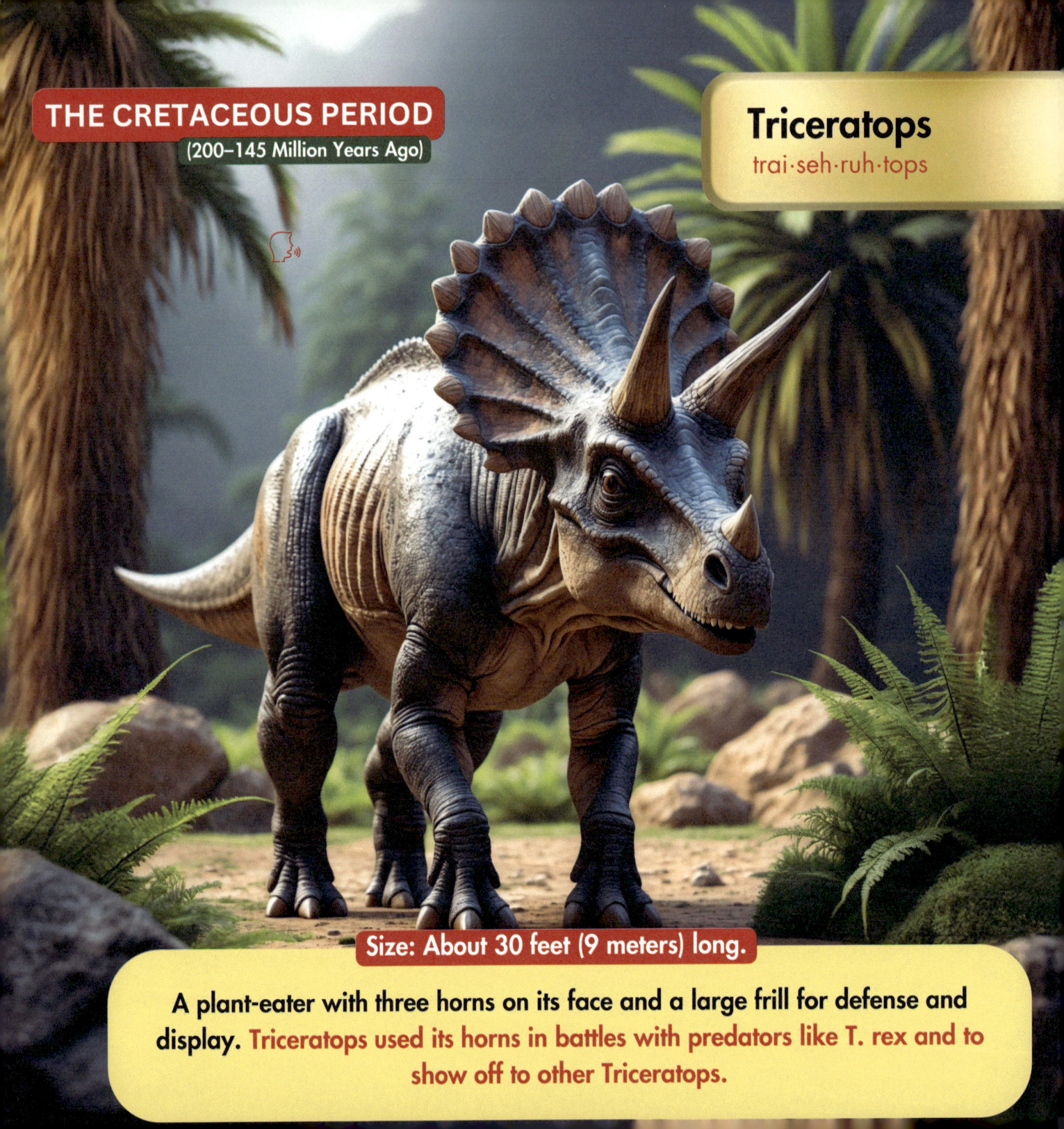

THE CRETACEOUS PERIOD
(200–145 Million Years Ago)

Triceratops
trai·seh·ruh·tops

Size: About 30 feet (9 meters) long.

A plant-eater with three horns on its face and a large frill for defense and display. Triceratops used its horns in battles with predators like T. rex and to show off to other Triceratops.

THE CRETACEOUS PERIOD
(200–145 Million Years Ago)

Velociraptor
vuh·lo·suh·rap·taw

Size: About 6 feet (2 meters) long.

A small, fast predator that hunted in packs, using its sharp claws to capture prey. **Velociraptors were covered in feathers, making them more bird-like than reptiles!**

THE CRETACEOUS PERIOD
(200–145 Million Years Ago)

Spinosaurus
spai·nuh·saw·ruhs

Size: About 50 feet (15 meters) long.

The largest carnivorous dinosaur, Spinosaurus hunted fish and lived near rivers and swamps. It had a distinctive sail on its back. Spinosaurus is the first known swimming dinosaur.

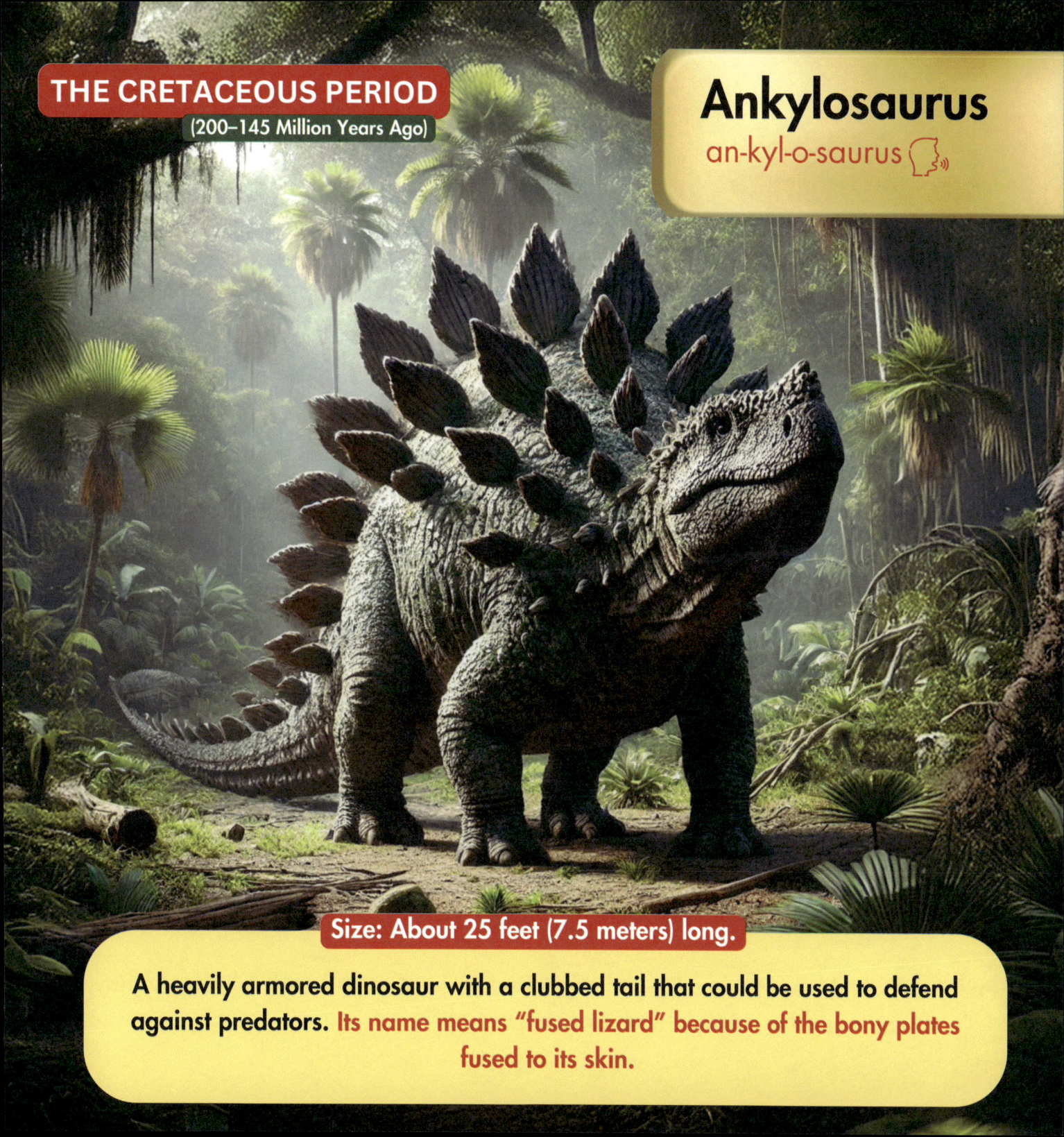

THE CRETACEOUS PERIOD
(200–145 Million Years Ago)

Ankylosaurus
an-kyl-o-saurus

Size: About 25 feet (7.5 meters) long.

A heavily armored dinosaur with a clubbed tail that could be used to defend against predators. *Its name means "fused lizard" because of the bony plates fused to its skin.*

Parasaurolophus
par-ah-sawr-ol-uh-fus

THE CRETACEOUS PERIOD
(200–145 Million Years Ago)

Size: About 33 feet (10 meters) long.

A plant-eater known for its long, tube-like crest on its head, which may have been used to make sounds or attract mates. Its crest could act like a built-in trumpet, allowing it to "honk" loudly.

THE CRETACEOUS PERIOD
(200–145 Million Years Ago)

Iguanodon
ih-gwah-nuh-don

Size: About 33 feet (10 meters) long.

A plant-eater with thumb spikes for defense and a flexible diet that helped it thrive. Iguanodon was one of the first dinosaurs ever discovered and named!

Therizinosaurus

ther-izinosaurus

THE CRETACEOUS PERIOD
(200–145 Million Years Ago)

Size: About 33 feet (10 meters) long.

A bizarre-looking herbivore with long, sharp claws that could grow up to 3 feet (1 meter) long. Despite its frightening claws, it likely used them to pull down plants for eating. Its name means "scythe lizard" because of its claw shape, making it one of the most unique-looking dinosaurs of the Cretaceous Period.

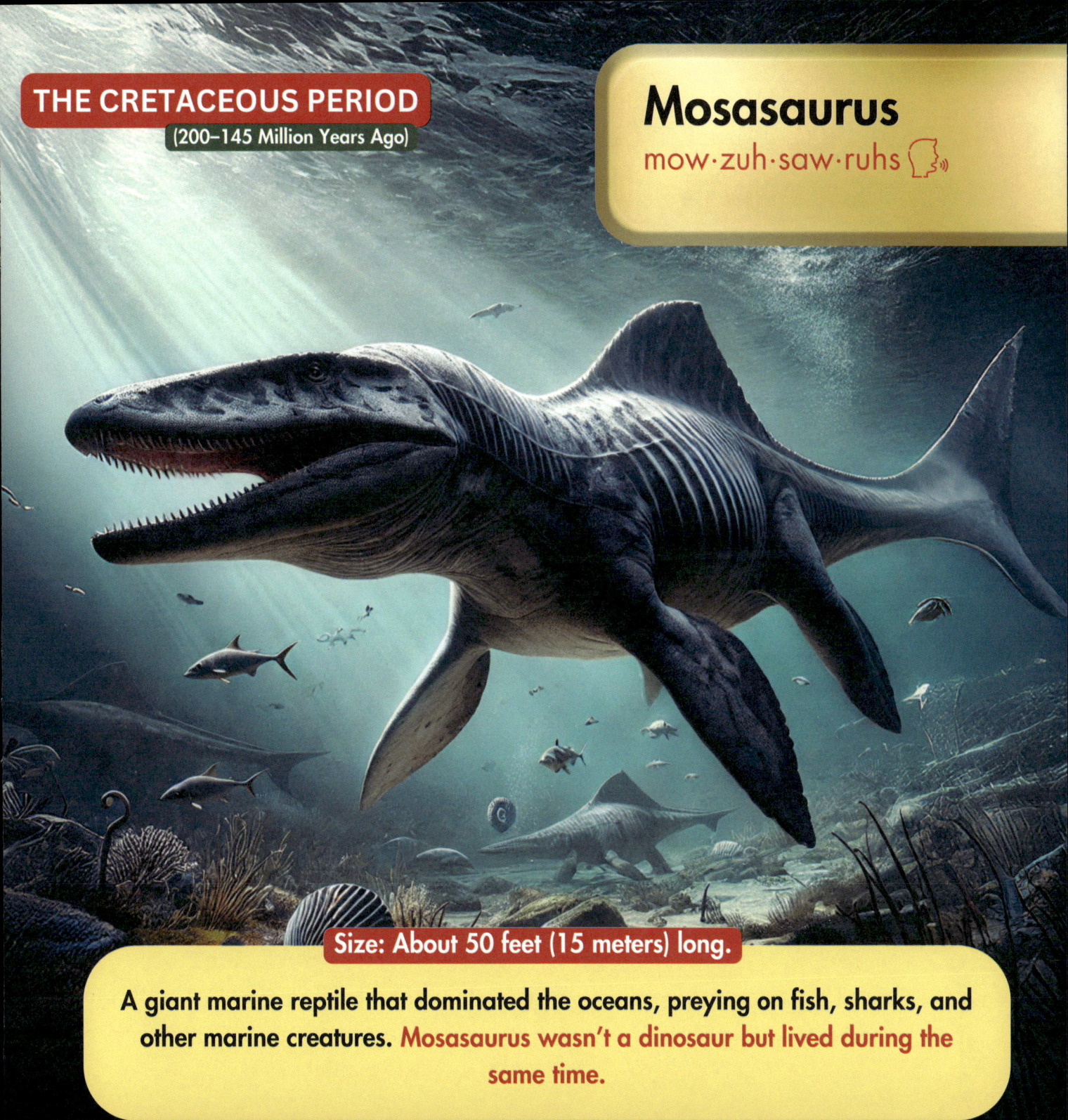

THE CRETACEOUS PERIOD
(200–145 Million Years Ago)

Mosasaurus
mow·zuh·saw·ruhs

Size: About 50 feet (15 meters) long.

A giant marine reptile that dominated the oceans, preying on fish, sharks, and other marine creatures. *Mosasaurus wasn't a dinosaur but lived during the same time.*

THE CRETACEOUS PERIOD
(200–145 Million Years Ago)

Argentinosaurus
ar-genti-nosaurus

Size: Up to 100 feet (30 meters) long.

One of the largest dinosaurs ever, this plant-eater had a massive, long body and a towering neck. Its weight was estimated to be around 100 tons—equivalent to 14 African elephants!

Chapter 4: Dinosaur Superpowers

Dinosaurs were like the superheroes of their time, with incredible features that helped them survive in a tough world. Let's discover some of their amazing abilities and see how they ruled the land!

1. Armor and Shields
2. Speed and Agility
3. Giant Jaws and Sharp Teeth
4. Flying High
5. Long Necks and Super Size
6. Camouflage and Disguises

1. Armor and Shields 🛡

Some dinosaurs were like walking fortresses, covered in tough armor to protect them from hungry predators.

ANKYLOSAURUS

This tank-like dino had bony plates all over its body and a clubbed tail that could knock out enemies. Imagine a prehistoric knight in shining armor!

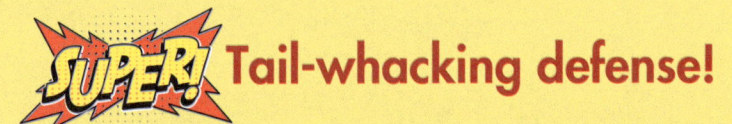

SUPER! Tail-whacking defense!

Ankylosaurus' tail club could break bones with one swing.

STEGOSAURUS

Stegosaurus had plates running down its back that weren't just for show—they helped regulate its body temperature and might have scared off predators.

SUPER! Spiky tail and flashy plates!

The spikes on its tail were called a "thagomizer."

2. Speed and Agility 🏃

Not all dinosaurs were big and slow. Some were built for speed and could outrun their predators.

VELOCIRAPTOR

These fast and smart hunters could zip through forests and outmaneuver prey. Their curved claws gave them a big advantage.

SUPER! Quick attacks and sharp claws!

Velociraptors were about the size of a turkey—but much scarier!

GALLIMIMUS

This dino, nicknamed the "ostrich mimic," had long legs for running at lightning speed. It probably relied on speed to escape predators.

SUPER! Outrunning danger!

Gallimimus could run over 30 miles per hour—faster than most cars in a city!

4. Flying High

Some dinosaurs (or their relatives) ruled the skies, gliding or flapping their wings to escape danger or catch prey.

PTERANODON

With a wingspan as wide as a school bus, this flying reptile (not technically a dinosaur) soared over the seas, hunting fish.

SUPER! Amazing gliding abilities!

Pteranodon's crest might have helped it steer while flying.

MICRORAPTOR

This tiny, feathered dino could glide between trees, making it the ninja of the forest.

SUPER! Stealthy gliding!

Microraptor had feathers on its legs too—it was like a flying squirrel with wings!

5. Long Necks and Super Size

With its towering neck, Brachiosaurus could reach leaves no other dinosaur could. It didn't even need to compete for food!

BRACHIOSAURUS

With its towering neck, Brachiosaurus could reach leaves no other dinosaur could. It didn't even need to compete for food!

SUPER! Sky-high reach!

Brachiosaurus could eat up to 880 pounds of food a day. That's like munching on 3,500 apples!

ARGENTINOSAURUS

The heavyweight champion of the dino world, this plant-eater was as long as four school buses and weighed more than 10 elephants.

SUPER! Massive size and strength!

Its footprint was as big as a bathtub!

6. Camouflage and Disguises

Some dinosaurs had built-in camouflage to hide from predators or sneak up on prey.

CARNOTAURUS

This meat-eating dino had tiny arms but blended perfectly into its surroundings with its scaly skin.

SUPER! Master of disguise!

Its name means "meat-eating bull" because of its bull-like horns.

CRYOLOPHOSAURUS

Known as the "frozen dinosaur" (discovered in Antarctica), it might have had colors to blend into snowy landscapes.

SUPER! Arctic camouflage!

Cryolophosaurus had a unique crest on its head that looked like a Spanish comb

Dino Detective Activity!

1. If you could have one dino superpower, what would it be and why?
2. Draw your favorite dinosaur using its superpower in action!

Chapter 5: How Did Dinosaurs Disappear?

Dinosaurs ruled the Earth for millions of years, but about 66 million years ago, their incredible reign came to an end. What could have wiped out these mighty creatures? Let's explore the mystery of the dino extinction!

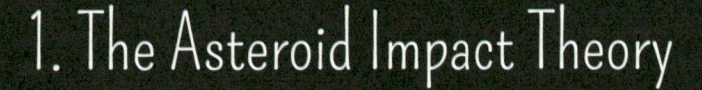

1. The Asteroid Impact Theory
2. Volcanoes Gone Wild
3. Climate Change and a Tough Environment

The Asteroid Impact Theory

The most popular theory is that a giant asteroid crashed into Earth near what is now the Yucatán Peninsula in Mexico. This event caused massive destruction that made it nearly impossible for dinosaurs to survive.

The Crash Heard Around the World
The asteroid was about 6 miles wide—that's as big as a mountain! When it hit, it created a crater over 90 miles wide. The impact was so powerful that it released energy equal to billions of atomic bombs.

What Happened Next?
- Fires broke out across the planet.
- Dust and ash filled the sky, blocking sunlight for months or even years.
- Temperatures dropped, plants stopped growing, and the food chain collapsed.

FUN FACT The giant crater left by the asteroid is called the Chicxulub Crater, and scientists discovered it in the 1970s.

Volcanoes Gone Wild 🌋

Another theory suggests that massive volcanic eruptions in a region called the Deccan Traps (in present-day India) contributed to the extinction.

Lava, Ash, and Gases

For thousands of years, volcanoes erupted nonstop, covering the land with lava and filling the atmosphere with toxic gases. This made the air hard to breathe and changed the climate.

FUN FACT: The volcanic eruptions might have released so much carbon dioxide that Earth's climate became too hot for many animals to survive.

Climate Change and a Tough Environment ❄️🔥

Even before the asteroid or volcanoes, Earth's environment was changing. The climate was becoming less stable, with extreme heat in some areas and cold in others. These changes made life harder for dinosaurs.

Rising Seas & Colder Temperatures

Oceans were rising and flooding dino habitats, reducing the land they could live on. Some scientists think dinosaurs couldn't adapt to colder weather as the planet cooled down.

FUN FACT: Dinosaurs that survived likely evolved into birds, which could adapt to changing climates.

What About the Survivors?

While most dinosaurs didn't make it, some of their relatives survived. Birds are considered modern dinosaurs because they share a lot of traits, like hollow bones and feathers. So, in a way, dinosaurs never really disappeared—they just evolved into something new!

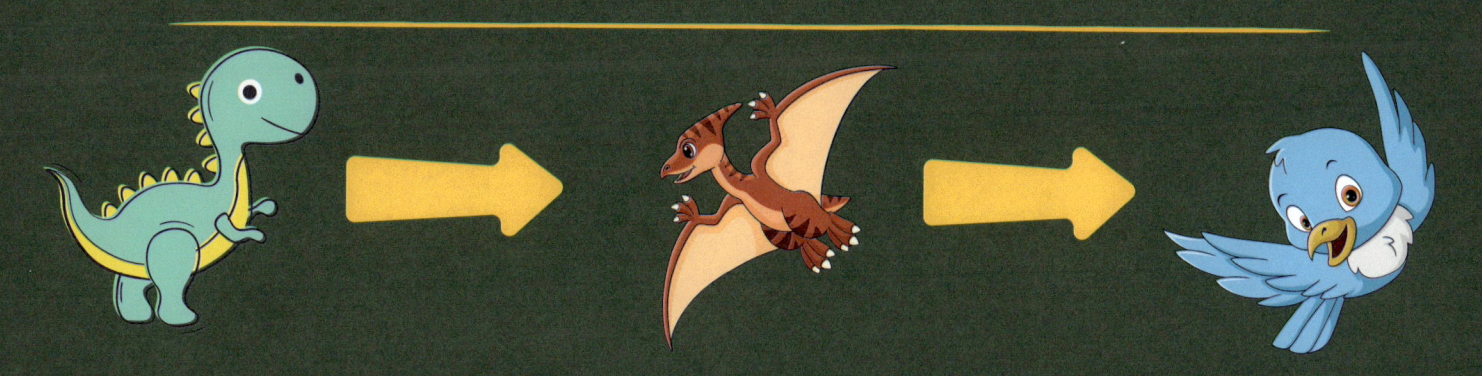

Mystery Solved? Maybe Not!

Scientists are still learning about what really happened, and it's possible that several factors worked together to end the Age of Dinosaurs. The asteroid, volcanoes, and climate change might have all played a part.

Dino Detective Activity!

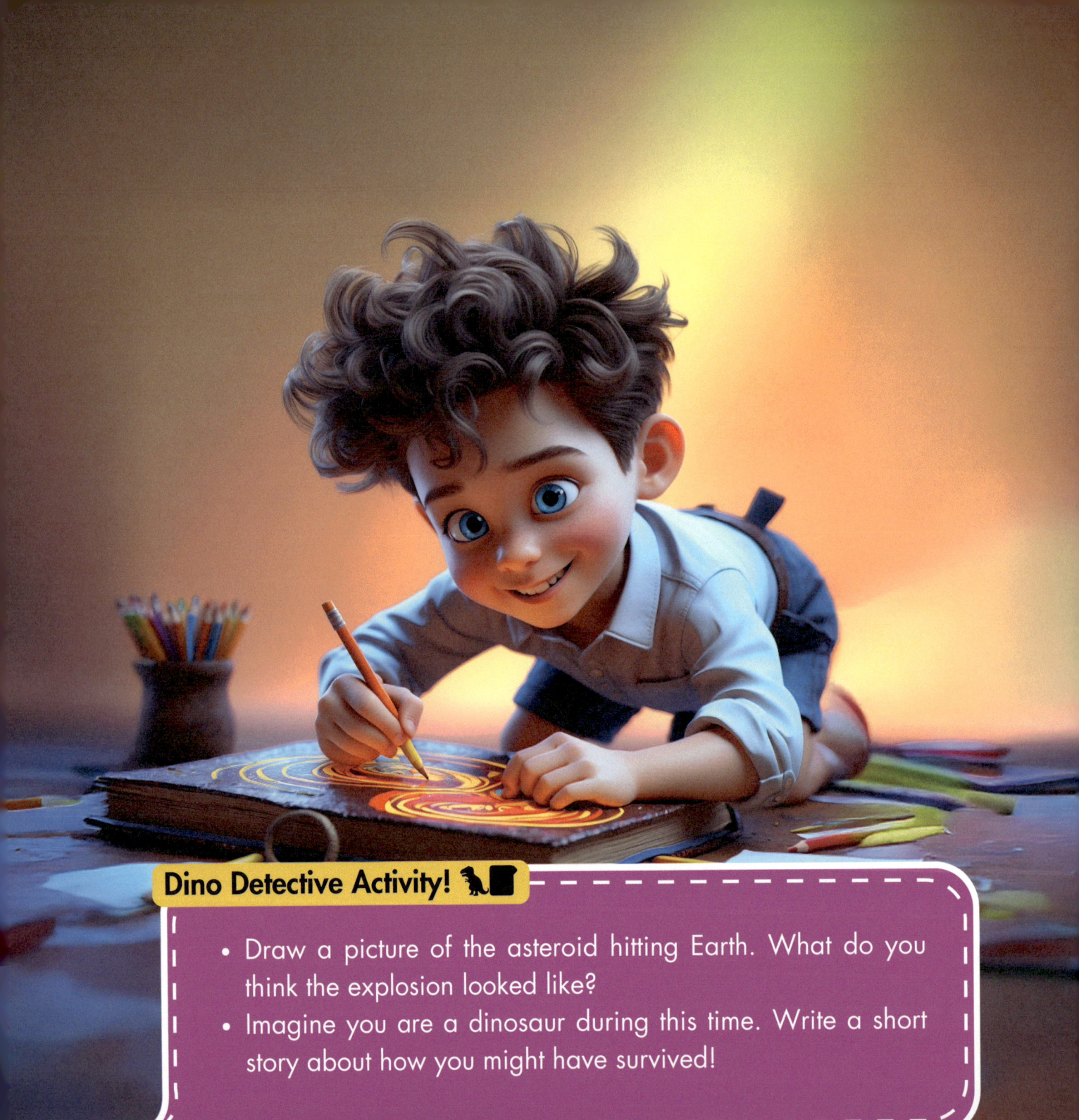

- Draw a picture of the asteroid hitting Earth. What do you think the explosion looked like?
- Imagine you are a dinosaur during this time. Write a short story about how you might have survived!

Chapter 6: Fossils and Paleontology

How do we know so much about dinosaurs when they lived millions of years ago? The answer is fossils—nature's way of leaving behind clues from the past. Paleontologists are the scientists who study these clues to unlock the secrets of dinosaurs. Let's dig in!

What Are Fossils?

Fossils are the remains or traces of ancient plants and animals that have been preserved in rocks. They can be bones, teeth, shells, or even footprints!

How Are Fossils Formed?

When a dinosaur died, its body might get buried in mud or sand. Over time, more layers of earth piled up, and the soft parts of the body decayed. The bones and teeth hardened into stone, creating a fossil.

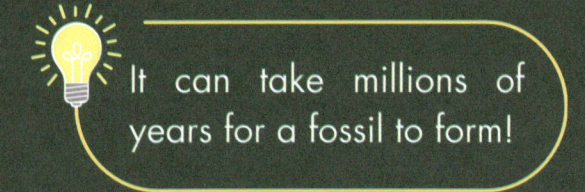

💡 It can take millions of years for a fossil to form!

Types of Fossils

Body Fossils
Actual parts of the dinosaur, like bones or teeth.

Trace Fossils
Footprints, eggs, or even dino poop (called coprolites).

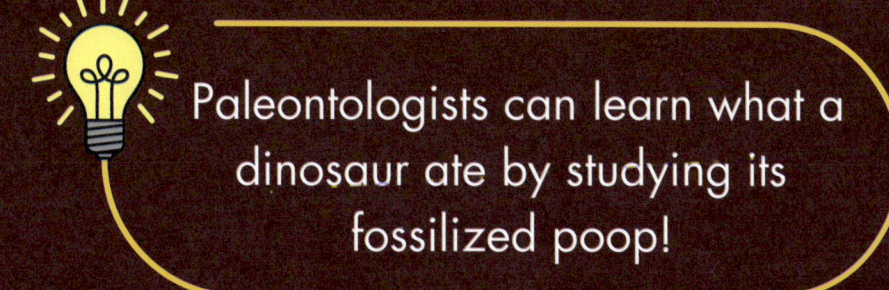

💡 Paleontologists can learn what a dinosaur ate by studying its fossilized poop!

What Do Paleontologists Do?

Paleontologists are like detectives of the past. They study fossils to understand how dinosaurs lived, moved, and even what they ate.

How They Find Fossils

Paleontologists search in places where ancient rocks are exposed, like deserts and cliffs. They carefully dig out fossils using tools like brushes and chisels to avoid damaging them.

What Happens Next?

After digging up fossils, paleontologists take them to a lab to clean and study. Sometimes, they use computer models to recreate how dinosaurs looked or moved.

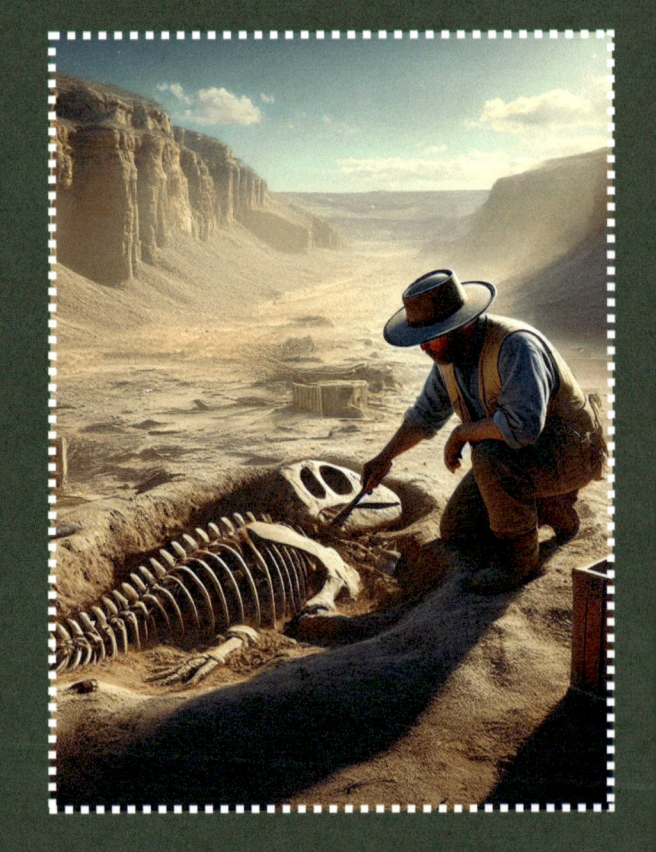

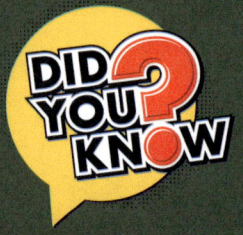

DID YOU KNOW? The Gobi Desert in Mongolia is one of the best places to find dinosaur fossils! Scientists discovered that many dinosaurs had feathers by examining tiny details in fossils under a microscope.

What Can Fossils Tell Us? 🧩

Fossils are like puzzle pieces that help us imagine what the world was like millions of years ago. Here's what they reveal:

Size and Shape
Fossils show how big or small a dinosaur was.

How They Moved
Fossilized footprints can tell us if a dino ran, walked, or even swam.

What They Ate
Teeth and coprolites reveal if a dinosaur was a plant-eater, meat-eater, or both.

Where They Lived
Fossils found in certain rocks can tell us about the dinosaur's habitat.

The Most Amazing Fossil Finds! 🏆

Sue the T. rex
The largest and most complete T. rex fossil ever found, now displayed in a museum in Chicago.

Dinosaur Mummies
Some fossils preserve not just bones but also skin and soft tissue.

Fossilized Eggs
These help scientists understand how dinosaurs raised their babies.

Dino Detective Activity!

- Draw your own fossil! Imagine what a dinosaur footprint or bone might look like.
- Pretend you're a paleontologist and write about your dream fossil discovery. What would you find?

Chapter 7: Dinosaurs in the Modern World

Did you know dinosaurs aren't completely gone? In a way, they're still with us today. Let's explore how dinosaurs live on in modern animals, science, and our everyday lives!

Dinosaurs Evolved into Birds 🐦

The next time you see a pigeon or a chicken, you're looking at a distant relative of the mighty dinosaurs! Scientists discovered that some small, feathered dinosaurs survived the extinction event 66 million years ago and eventually evolved into birds.

Feathers, Not Scales
Many dinosaurs, like Velociraptor and Microraptor, had feathers. This means modern birds are more closely related to dinosaurs than lizards or crocodiles.

A Living Link
The ostrich is one of the closest living relatives to dinosaurs. Its long legs, sharp claws, and speedy running might remind you of a Velociraptor!

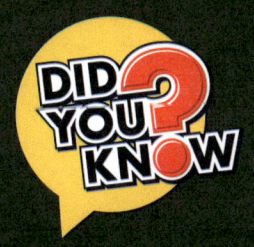

DID YOU KNOW? Birds have hollow bones, just like many dinosaurs, which makes them light enough to fly. Chickens share some DNA with the T. rex—so maybe think twice before teasing one!

What Dinosaurs Teach Us Today

Dinosaurs are more than ancient creatures—they help scientists understand how life on Earth changes over time.

Studying Extinction
By learning what caused the dinosaurs to disappear, scientists can better understand how to protect today's animals from extinction.

Bringing Dinosaurs Back?
Movies make us wonder: could we ever bring dinosaurs back to life? While cloning a real dinosaur isn't possible, scientists are studying ancient DNA to understand more about these creatures.

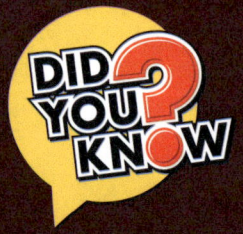

DID YOU KNOW? Some scientists think we're in the middle of another mass extinction caused by habitat loss and climate change. Some researchers are experimenting with "de-evolving" birds to recreate dinosaur-like traits!

Modern Dinosaur Discoveries

China's Feathered Fossils

Some of the best-preserved feathered dinosaurs, like Sinosauropteryx, were found in China. These discoveries prove that feathers were common in many dinosaur species.

Underwater Finds

Marine reptile fossils, like those of Mosasaurus, show us that the oceans were just as wild as the land during the Age of Dinosaurs.

DID YOU KNOW? The Mosasaurus wasn't technically a dinosaur but lived at the same time and could grow up to 50 feet long!

Dino Detective Activity!

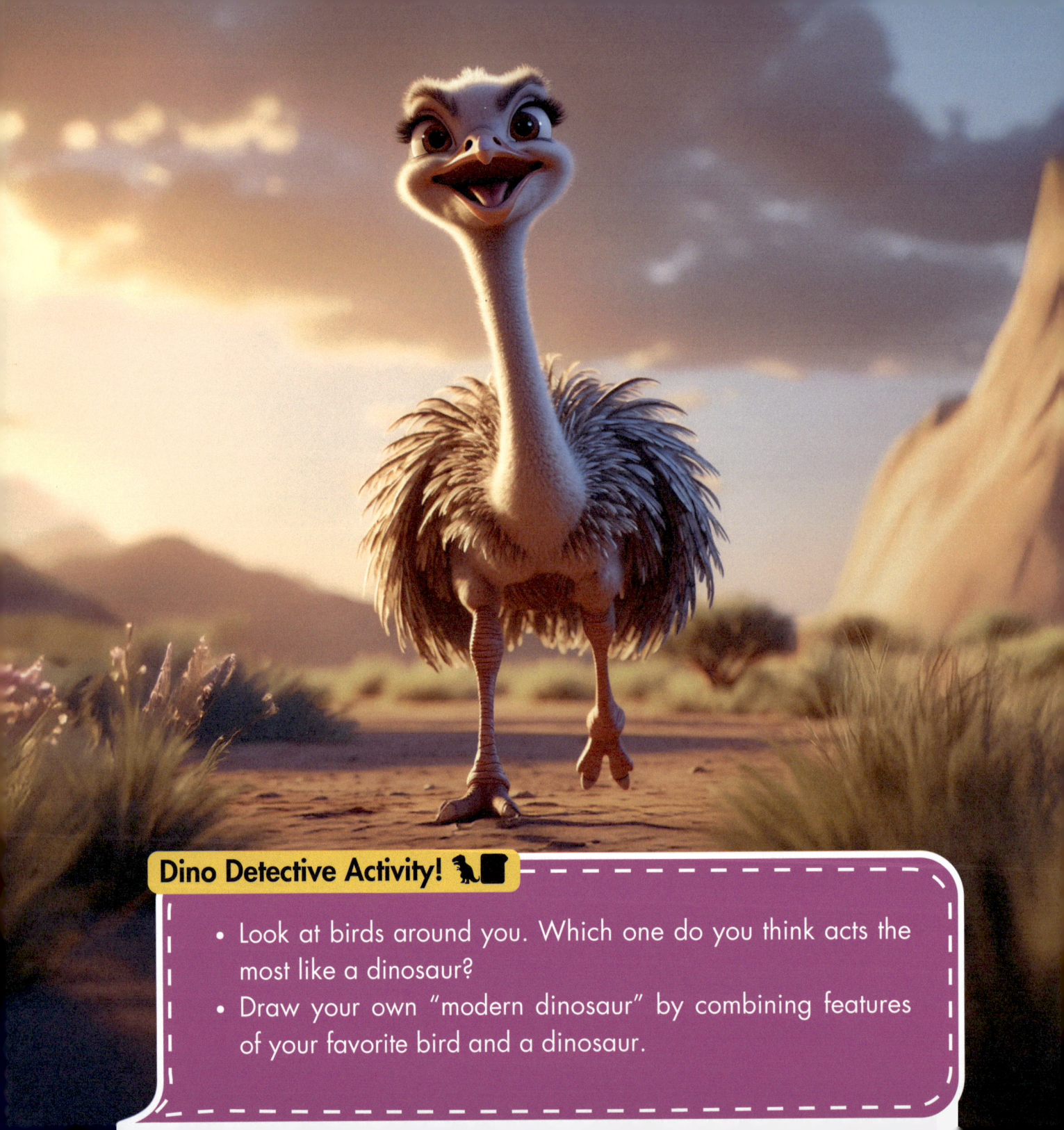

- Look at birds around you. Which one do you think acts the most like a dinosaur?
- Draw your own "modern dinosaur" by combining features of your favorite bird and a dinosaur.

Dinosaur Size Comparison

1. Size of a Dinosaur vs. a Human 🦖 vs. 👤

Dinosaur	Length	Height	How It Compares to a Human
Tyrannosaurus rex	40 feet (12 meters)	15 feet (4.5 meters)	As long as a school bus, as tall as a giraffe!
Velociraptor	6.5 feet (2 meters)	2 feet (0.6 meters)	About the size of a turkey, but way more dangerous!
Brachiosaurus	85 feet (26 meters)	40 feet (12 meters)	Longer than two buses and as tall as a four-story building.
Compsognathus	2.5 feet (0.7 meters)	1 foot (0.3 meters)	The size of a chicken. Cute, right?

2. Weight of a Dinosaur vs. a Modern Animal ⚖️

Dinosaur	Weight	Modern Comparison
Stegosaurus	5,500 pounds (2,500 kg)	About the same as an adult rhino.
Ankylosaurus	10,000 pounds (4,500 kg)	The weight of an armored truck!
Argentinosaurus	100,000 pounds (45,000 kg)	As heavy as 10 African elephants.
Microraptor	2 pounds (0.9 kg)	Lighter than a house cat.

3. Speed of Dinosaurs vs. Modern Animals 🚀

Dinosaur	Speed	Modern Comparison
Tyrannosaurus rex	20 mph (32 kph)	As fast as a cyclist.
Gallimimus	30 mph (48 kph)	As fast as a car in a city.
Velociraptor	25 mph (40 kph)	Faster than the fastest human sprinter.
Brachiosaurus	6 mph (9 kph)	About as fast as you walking briskly.

Dinosaur Size Comparison

4. Egg Size of Dinosaurs vs. Modern Animals

Dinosaur	Egg Size	Modern Comparison
Oviraptor	6 inches (15 cm)	About the size of a goose egg.
Titanosaurus	12 inches (30 cm)	As big as a basketball.
Maiasaura	8 inches (20 cm)	Larger than an ostrich egg.

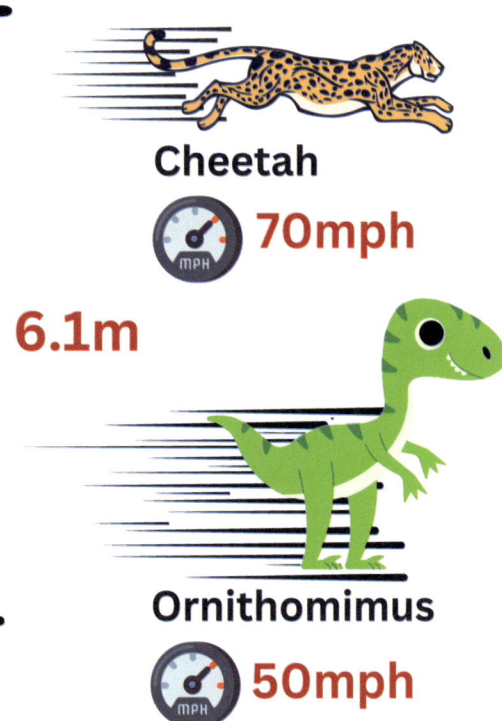

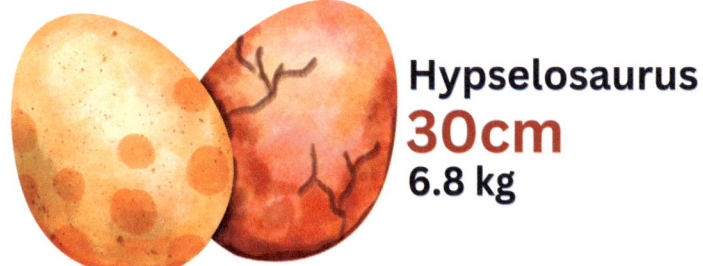

1.8m

6.1m

Cheetah 70mph

Ornithomimus 50mph

6 cm
60g

Hypselosaurus
30cm
6.8 kg

Fun Quizzes and Challenges 🦕

Which Dinosaur Are You?

Answer the questions below to find out which dinosaur matches your personality!

1. What's your favorite thing to eat?
2. a) Meat! Bring on the steak.
3. b) Leafy greens and veggies.
4. c) A mix of everything—I like variety.

How do you like to spend your day?

a) Exploring and hunting for new adventures.
b) Relaxing and enjoying the sunshine.
c) Running around with friends.

What's your special skill?

a) Being strong and brave.
b) Staying calm and steady.
c) Being quick and clever.

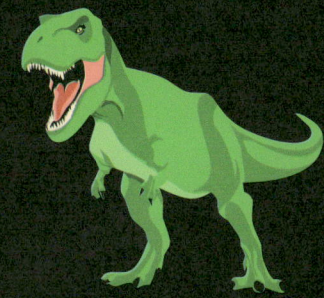

Mostly A: You're a T. rex! Bold, powerful, and ready for action.

Mostly B: You're a Brachiosaurus! Gentle, laid-back, and a lover of plants.

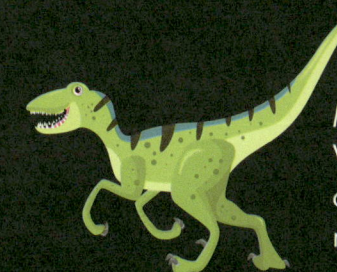

Mostly C: You're a Velociraptor! Fast, clever, and a little mischievous.

Dino Trivia Time!

Which dinosaur had three horns?

a) Triceratops
b) Stegosaurus
c) Allosaurus
(Answer: Triceratops)

What's the smallest dinosaur ever discovered?

a) Compsognathus
b) Argentinosaurus
c) T. rex
(Answer: Compsognathus)

What did Ankylosaurus use to defend itself?

a) Its horns
b) Its spiky tail
c) Its teeth
(Answer: Its spiky tail)

Dino Match-Up Challenge

Dinosaur	Description
T. rex	a) Had a long neck and ate plants
Brachiosaurus	b) Was the king of the carnivores
Velociraptor	c) Small and fast, hunted in packs

Answers:
T. rex   b
Brachiosaurus   a
Velociraptor   c

True or False?

Are these statements true or false?
- All dinosaurs lived at the same time. (False)
- Some dinosaurs had feathers. (True)
- Triceratops was a carnivore. (False)
- Dinosaurs evolved into modern birds. (True)

Dino Detective Scavenger Hunt

Look through your book or your surroundings to find:
- A shape that reminds you of a dinosaur footprint.
- A modern animal that looks like a dinosaur.
- The name of the largest dinosaur mentioned in the book.

Dino Detective Riddles

I'm big and strong, with teeth like knives. I hunt in packs to survive my life. Who am I? (Velociraptor)

I have three horns but don't eat meat. You'd find me munching plants as a tasty treat. Who am I? (Triceratops)

Experiments and Exploration

Make Your Own Volcano 🌋

Recreate the explosive world of the Jurassic Period with a simple, safe volcano experiment.

What You'll Need:
- A plastic bottle (small size works best)
- Baking soda
- Vinegar
- Dish soap (optional, for more bubbles)
- Red food coloring (optional, for lava effect)
- Modeling clay or papier-mâché to build the volcano shape

Instructions:
1. Build your volcano around the bottle using clay or papier-mâché, leaving the bottle's neck open at the top.
2. Add 2 tablespoons of baking soda inside the bottle.
3. Add a few drops of red food coloring and a squirt of dish soap.
4. Pour vinegar into the bottle and watch your volcano erupt!

Volcanoes were active during the Age of Dinosaurs, shaping the land where these creatures roamed.

Experiments and Exploration

Create a Fossil 🦴
Learn how fossils are made by making your own at home!

What You'll Need:
- Modeling clay or play dough
- Small toy dinosaur or leaf
- Plaster of Paris or flour and water paste

Instructions:
1. Flatten the clay into a small disc.
2. Press your toy dinosaur or leaf into the clay to leave an imprint.
3. Mix the plaster of Paris and pour it over the imprint. Let it dry.
4. Once dry, remove the clay to reveal your fossil!

Fossils help paleontologists learn about dinosaurs and their environment.

Measure a Dino 🦖
Visualize the size of your favorite dinosaurs with this interactive measuring activity.

What You'll Need:
- Measuring tape
- Sidewalk chalk (or string and markers if indoors)

Instructions:
1. Use the measuring tape to mark the length of a dinosaur (e.g., T. rex = 40 feet, Brachiosaurus = 85 feet).
2. Use chalk to draw the outline of the dinosaur's body.
3. Compare yourself to the dinosaur by standing next to your outline.

Experiments and Exploration

Dino Egg Hunt

Discover how paleontologists uncover dinosaur eggs!

What You'll Need:
- Plastic Easter eggs or small objects wrapped in aluminum foil
- Sand or flour in a large container or sandbox
- Small brushes (like paintbrushes)

Instructions:
1. Bury the eggs in the sand.
2. Pretend you're a paleontologist and use the brushes to carefully "excavate" the eggs without breaking them.
3. Examine your finds and imagine what kind of dinosaur might hatch from each egg.

Dino Shadow Art

Learn about how dinosaurs' shapes cast shadows.

What You'll Need:
- Dinosaur toys or cutouts
- A flashlight
- A blank wall or large sheet of paper

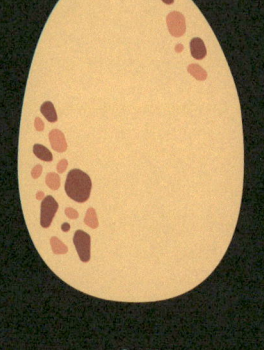

Instructions:
1. Shine the flashlight at the toy or cutout to create a shadow on the wall.
2. Trace the shadow on the paper or wall with a pencil.
3. Color in the shadow to create dino art!

Dino Jokes and Puns

Why Did the Dinosaur...?
- Why did the T. rex cross the road?
- To eat the chicken on the other side!

- Why did the Velociraptor sit on a fence?
- To get a bird's-eye view of dinner!

- Why did the Stegosaurus eat so much?
- Because it was a herbivore-it!

What Do You Call...?
- What do you call a dinosaur that sleeps all the time?
- **A dino-snore!**

- What do you call a dinosaur with a great vocabulary?
- **A thesaurus!**

- What do you call a T. rex who works out a lot?
- **Dino-sore!**

Knock, Knock!
- Knock, knock.
- Who's there?
- Dino.
- Dino who?
- Dino how long I've been waiting for you to open the door?

- Knock, knock.
- Who's there?
- Fossil.
- Fossil who?
- Fossil laugh, this joke is dino-mite!

Dino Detective Riddles
- I'm big and strong, with teeth like knives.
- I hunt in packs to survive my life.
- Who am I? (Velociraptor)

- I have three horns but don't eat meat.
- You'd find me munching plants as a tasty treat.
- Who am I? (Triceratops)

A Message to Our Dino Explorers

Congratulations, dino explorer! You've traveled millions of years back in time, met some of the most incredible creatures to ever walk the Earth, and uncovered the secrets of the dinosaur world. From the tiny Compsognathus to the towering Brachiosaurus, every dinosaur had a unique story, and now, you're part of their history, too!

But the adventure doesn't end here! Dinosaurs may be gone, but their legacy lives on in modern birds, fossils waiting to be discovered, and our imaginations. Keep exploring, asking questions, and learning about the amazing world around you—because just like a true paleontologist, there's always something new to uncover.

Thank you for joining me on this prehistoric journey. Now, go share your dino knowledge and maybe even teach someone how to roar like a T. rex! Until next time, keep stomping, roaring, and discovering!

The End 🦖✨

DINESH DECKKER
AUTHOR

Dinesh Deckker is a multifaceted author and educator with a rich academic background and extensive experience in creative writing and education. Holding a BSc Hons in Computer Science, a BA (Hons), and an MBA from prestigious institutions in the UK, Dinesh has dedicated his career to blending technology, education, and literature.

BA, MBA (UK), PhD (Student)

He has further honed his writing skills through a variety of specialized courses. His qualifications include:

- Children Acquiring Literacy Naturally from UC Santa Cruz, USA
- Creative Writing Specialization from Wesleyan University, USA
- Writing for Young Readers Commonwealth Education Trust
- Introduction to Early Childhood from The State University of New York
- Introduction to Psychology from Yale University
- Academic English: Writing Specialization University of California, Irvine,
- Writing and Editing Specialization from University of Michigan
- Writing and Editing: Word Choice University of Michigan
- Sharpened Visions: A Poetry Workshop from CalArts, USA
- Grammar and Punctuation from University of California, Irvine, USA
- Teaching Writing Specialization from Johns Hopkins University
- Advanced Writing from University of California, Irvine, USA
- English for Journalism from University of Pennsylvania, USA
- Creative Writing: The Craft of Character from Wesleyan University, USA
- Creative Writing: The Craft of Setting from Wesleyan University
- Creative Writing: The Craft of Plot from Wesleyan University, USA
- Creative Writing: The Craft of Style from Wesleyan University, USA

Dinesh's diverse educational background and commitment to lifelong learning have equipped him with a deep understanding of various writing styles and educational techniques. His works often reflect his passion for storytelling, education, and technology, making him a versatile and engaging author.

SUBHASHINI SUMANASEKARA
AUTHOR

With more than 20 years of expertise, Subhashini Sumanasekara is a renowned ICT educator committed to mentoring students from a variety of backgrounds. Her experience in the industry is further enhanced by her Master of Science in Strategic IT Management.

BSc, MSc (UK), PhD (Student)